The 52-Week Romance Journal

Welcome to The 52-Week Romance Journal!

This inspirational journal will give you 52 fun and unique weekly activities designed specifically to add a whole new level of romance to your life. Plus, the specially crafted follow up questions will help support you in your journey and reinforce the amazing progress and growth you're enjoying.

The reason this journal doesn't start on a fixed date is because neither does life. We all move at our own pace and time. Your commitment to adding more romance to your life might not begin on January 1st. We all evolve and grow at our own pace throughout the year. Every 52-Week Journal is designed to work with you on your own time.

Whenever you're ready, so is this journal.

You can go in the order of the pages, repeat pages that specifically connect with you, or skip ahead to find new exercises and activities that speak to you where you are at any given time.

It's all up to you!

Romance is about inspiration and freedom from life's many constraints. This journal's goal is to help inspire you to create a life rich with romance whenever you want.

As you'll see, many of the activities in this journal are designed to be done on your own. Others may be shared with someone special. The ultimate goal is to empower you to create the romance-filled life of your dreams.

You might find yourself reaching for this journal every morning without fail. You might want to take the occasional break. With the 52-Week Journal you always set your own rules.

So, open up this journal, and open up your heart. It's time to fill your life with all of the romance you desire.

Week 1

Start a Romance Vision
Board and add something to
it every day.

To love for the sake of being
loved is human, but to love for the
sake of loving is angelic.

~ Alphonse de Lamartine

Date: ───────────

What was the first thing you added to the board?

───────────────────────────────────────
───────────────────────────────────────
───────────────────────────────────────
───────────────────────────────────────
───────────────────────────────────────
───────────────────────────────────────

Did you hang the board somewhere you see it everyday?

───────────────────────────────────────
───────────────────────────────────────
───────────────────────────────────────
───────────────────────────────────────
───────────────────────────────────────
───────────────────────────────────────

Did you share the board with anyone?

───────────────────────────────────────
───────────────────────────────────────
───────────────────────────────────────
───────────────────────────────────────
───────────────────────────────────────
───────────────────────────────────────
───────────────────────────────────────

Week 2

Learn three sexy phrases in another language and slip them into your conversations all week.

J'ai eu un coup de foudre.

Literally translates to "bolt of lightning." However in French, the language of love, it figuratively means "love at first sight."

Date: ───────────

What phrases did you learn?

───────────────────────────────
───────────────────────────────
───────────────────────────────
───────────────────────────────
───────────────────────────────
───────────────────────────────

When did you use them?

───────────────────────────────
───────────────────────────────
───────────────────────────────
───────────────────────────────
───────────────────────────────

What was the reaction you got when you used them?

───────────────────────────────
───────────────────────────────
───────────────────────────────
───────────────────────────────
───────────────────────────────
───────────────────────────────
───────────────────────────────

Week 3

Sit outside to people watch and make up romantic stories about them.

Listen with ears of tolerance! See through the eyes of compassion! Speak with the language of love.

~ Rumi

Date: ───────

What did the people look like?

───────────────────────
───────────────────────
───────────────────────
───────────────────────
───────────────────────
───────────────────────
───────────────────────
───────────────────────
───────────────────────

What were some of the favorite storylines you made up?

───────────────────────
───────────────────────
───────────────────────
───────────────────────
───────────────────────
───────────────────────
───────────────────────
───────────────────────
───────────────────────
───────────────────────
───────────────────────

Week 4

Create 10 fun, romantic, and sexy questions to ask someone special.

Never close your lips to those whom you have already opened your heart.

~ CHARLES DICKENS

Date: ———————

What was on your list?

_____
_____
_____
_____
_____
_____
_____
_____
_____

Were you surprised by any of the answers?

_____
_____
_____
_____
_____
_____
_____
_____
_____
_____

Week 5

Buy a beautiful greeting card from the Love section, frame it and hang it on your wall.

Romance is the glamour which turns the dust of everyday life into a golden haze.

~ Elinor Glyn

Date: ―――――――

What made this card the one you chose?

―――――――――――――――――――――――――
―――――――――――――――――――――――――
―――――――――――――――――――――――――
―――――――――――――――――――――――――
―――――――――――――――――――――――――
―――――――――――――――――――――――――

Where did you hang it?

―――――――――――――――――――――――――
―――――――――――――――――――――――――
―――――――――――――――――――――――――
―――――――――――――――――――――――――
―――――――――――――――――――――――――
―――――――――――――――――――――――――

How did it make you feel to see it every day?

―――――――――――――――――――――――――
―――――――――――――――――――――――――
―――――――――――――――――――――――――
―――――――――――――――――――――――――
―――――――――――――――――――――――――
―――――――――――――――――――――――――
―――――――――――――――――――――――――

Week 6

*Write down a secret desire and work on
a plan to make it a reality.*

The very essence of romance is uncertainty.

~ OSCAR WILDE

Date: ———————

What is the secret desire?

_____
_____
_____
_____
_____
_____

Did you tell anyone about it?

_____
_____
_____
_____
_____
_____

What steps have you taken to make it happen?

_____
_____
_____
_____
_____
_____
_____

Week 7

Wear fancy, silky soft pajamas to bed.

One study showed that more sex happened per week when sleeping on silk sheets.

Date: ───────

What kind of pajamas did you get?

_____
_____
_____
_____
_____
_____

How did wearing the pajamas make you feel?

_____
_____
_____
_____
_____
_____

If someone else saw the pajamas, what was their reaction?

_____
_____
_____
_____
_____
_____

Week 8

Get cozy in front of a fireplace. If you don't have one at home, find a restaurant or hotel lobby that has one. Or safely build a fire outdoors.

Studies have shown that physical contact releases a hormone called oxytocin, sometimes called "the love hormone" that increases pair-bonding.

Date: ───────

Where was the fireplace?

_____
_____
_____
_____
_____

How did you feel while cozied up in front of the fire?

_____
_____
_____
_____
_____

What did you do afterwards?

_____
_____
_____
_____
_____
_____

Week 9

Mail a special someone a romantic card with a sweet message written inside.

Only one life, that soon is past. Only what's done with love will last.

~Unknown

Date: ───────────

Who did you mail the card to?

_____
_____
_____
_____
_____

What did the message say inside?

_____
_____
_____
_____
_____

Did you write anything else inside the card?

_____
_____
_____
_____
_____
_____
_____

Week 10

Add scents you love to your bedroom with a diffuser and essential oils.

Research suggests that citrus scents — specifically orange essential oil — helps alleviate stress and anxiety.

Date: ───────────

What scents did you try?

_____
_____
_____
_____
_____
_____

What scent was your favorite?

_____
_____
_____
_____
_____
_____

How did the scents make you feel?

_____
_____
_____
_____
_____
_____
_____

Week 11

Stroll through a beautiful, lush outdoor space and make a conscious effort to admire the beauty around you.

Spending just 15 minutes per day outside exposes us to nature's vitamin D through sunlight, ideally protecting us from feeling sad.

Date: _____

Where did you go?

_____
_____
_____
_____
_____
_____

Did it make you want to go there again?

_____
_____
_____
_____
_____
_____

How did you feel afterwards?

_____
_____
_____
_____
_____
_____
_____
_____

Week 12

Give someone special an extra long hug every day this week.

Where love is concerned, too much is not even enough.

~ Pierre Beaumarchais

Date: ―――――――

How did it make you feel?

―――――――――――――――――――――――
―――――――――――――――――――――――
―――――――――――――――――――――――
―――――――――――――――――――――――
―――――――――――――――――――――――
―――――――――――――――――――――――

How do you think they felt?

―――――――――――――――――――――――
―――――――――――――――――――――――
―――――――――――――――――――――――
―――――――――――――――――――――――
―――――――――――――――――――――――

Are there other people you want to try this with?

―――――――――――――――――――――――
―――――――――――――――――――――――
―――――――――――――――――――――――
―――――――――――――――――――――――
―――――――――――――――――――――――
―――――――――――――――――――――――
―――――――――――――――――――――――

Week 13

Have sexy French music playing in the background when you cook dinner.

Sexy

/ˈseksē/ *adjective*

Sexually attractive or stimulating

Date: ―――――――――

What was your favorite song?

_____
_____
_____
_____
_____
_____

How did it make you feel listening to it?

_____
_____
_____
_____
_____
_____

Are there songs in other languages you want to listen to now?

_____
_____
_____
_____
_____
_____
_____

Week 14

Have a picnic in the park with all your favorite foods.

When we love - we grow.

~ Theophile Gautier

Date: ———————

Where did you have your picnic?

_____
_____
_____
_____
_____

What foods did you have?

_____
_____
_____
_____
_____

Do you think you'll try this again?

_____
_____
_____
_____
_____
_____

Week 15

Read a romantic novel out loud.

Love is a breach in the walls, a broken gate,
where that comes in that shall not go out again.

~Rupert Brooke

Date: ———————

What book did you read?

_____
_____
_____
_____
_____
_____

Did it make you feel funny or exciting to read it aloud?

_____
_____
_____
_____
_____
_____

Did you read the whole book?

_____
_____
_____
_____
_____
_____

Week 16

Watch a romantic movie and share your favorite moments.

Every night and every morning close your eyes and take three deep breaths and say out loud - "Love attracts love, and my heart is full of love"

Date: ───────────

What movie did you watch?

_____
_____
_____
_____
_____
_____

What were your favorite moments?

_____
_____
_____
_____
_____
_____

Were you surprised by any of the shared favorite moments?

_____
_____
_____
_____
_____
_____
_____

Week 17

Plan a fantasy romantic dream vacation with someone special.

No man truly has joy unless he lives in love.

~ St. Thomas Aquinas

Date: ———————

Where did you plan to go?

_____
_____
_____
_____
_____
_____
_____
_____
_____

How can you make this dream trip, or at least part of it, a reality?

_____
_____
_____
_____
_____
_____
_____
_____
_____
_____
_____
_____

Week 18

Decorate your bedroom for romance
with lavish bedding, pillows or
a flowing canopy.

A British survey showed that people with
purple sheets or bedroom furniture had the
more sex per week compared to other colors.
Fair warning, gray sheets inspired the least
amount of sex.

Date: ―――――――

What décor changes did you make?

―――――――――――――――――――――――
―――――――――――――――――――――――
―――――――――――――――――――――――
―――――――――――――――――――――――
―――――――――――――――――――――――

Were you excited to go to bed after you decorated your room?

―――――――――――――――――――――――
―――――――――――――――――――――――
―――――――――――――――――――――――
―――――――――――――――――――――――
―――――――――――――――――――――――

Do you feel like it changed the mood in the bedroom?

―――――――――――――――――――――――
―――――――――――――――――――――――
―――――――――――――――――――――――
―――――――――――――――――――――――
―――――――――――――――――――――――
―――――――――――――――――――――――

Week 19

Eat a fancy breakfast in bed. Use cotton
napkins and add a flower in a vase
to your tray.

Every night and every morning, close your eyes
and take three deep breaths and say out loud
"I am fully open to receiving and giving love."

Date: ───────

What breakfast was served?

_____
_____
_____
_____
_____

Was it fun eating in bed?

_____
_____
_____
_____
_____

Do you think you'll make this a regular once a week thing?

_____
_____
_____
_____
_____
_____

Week 20

Create a collage of your favorite photos where you love how you look.

You yourself as much as anybody in the entire universe deserve your love and affection.

~ Gautama The Lord Buddha

Date: ───────────

When were the majority of the photos taken?

_____
_____
_____
_____
_____

Did you hang the collage up somewhere it could be seen regularly?

_____
_____
_____
_____
_____

Did you share the collage with friends or on social media? If so, what was the response?

_____
_____
_____
_____
_____

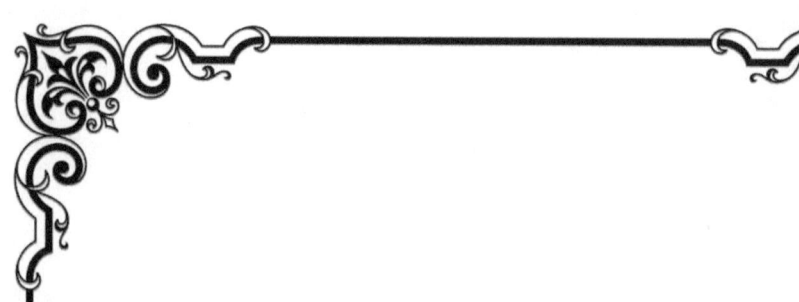

Week 21

Cuddle up and binge-watch an entire season of a romantic TV show.

There is no remedy for love but to love more.

~ Henry David Thoreau

Date: _____

What show did you watch?

_____
_____
_____
_____
_____
_____
_____
_____
_____
_____

What were your favorite episodes, and why?

_____
_____
_____
_____
_____
_____
_____
_____
_____
_____
_____
_____

Week 22

Meet someone special at a coffee shop
and pretend you are on a first date.
Ask questions about each other,
tell stories and flirt, flirt, flirt.

Studies have shown that being a good listener
leads to stronger relationships.

Date: ───────

Where did you go?

_____
_____
_____
_____
_____
_____

Was it fun or awkward?

_____
_____
_____
_____
_____
_____

Did you actually learn anything new about your "date?"

_____
_____
_____
_____
_____
_____
_____

Week 23

Take a bubble bath by candlelight. Add scented oils and relax to love songs.

Come live in my heart and pay no rent.

~ Samuel Lover

Date: ———————

Did the bath make you feel relaxed or invigorated?

_____
_____
_____
_____
_____
_____

What kind of mood were you in after the bath?

_____
_____
_____
_____
_____
_____

Will you make this a semi-regular thing from now on?

_____
_____
_____
_____
_____
_____
_____

Week 24

Plan a party where you and someone
special read sweet toasts aloud
to each other.

Every night and every morning, close your eyes
and take three deep breaths and say out loud
"I am grateful and thankful for
our love connection."

Date: ───────

What was your toast?

_____
_____
_____
_____
_____
_____

How did the party go over?

_____
_____
_____
_____
_____
_____

What was your favorite part about the toasts?

_____
_____
_____
_____
_____
_____
_____

Week 25

Print a sexy, happy picture of you smiling
and tape it to your bathroom mirror.

Having high self-esteem often leads to having
longer and more successful relationships.

Date: ───────

What picture did you choose?

_____
_____
_____
_____
_____
_____

How did you feel seeing that picture every day?

_____
_____
_____
_____
_____
_____

Are there more pictures you now plan on posting on the mirror?

_____
_____
_____
_____
_____
_____
_____

Week 26

Sing love songs out loud with
someone special.

Studies have shown that listening to music
can reduce stress.

Date: ―――――

What songs did you sing?

_____
_____
_____
_____
_____

Which one was your most favorite, and why?

_____
_____
_____
_____
_____

Was it fun and exciting or did you feel silly?

_____
_____
_____
_____
_____
_____

Week 27

Create a signature drink with your special someone and invite friends over to try it.

Cleopatra, known for her seductive beauty, had a signature lipstick made for her, made from a combination of crushed ants and deep red carmine beetles.

Date: ———————

What was in your drink?

_____
_____
_____
_____
_____
_____

Did you give your drink a name? And what names did you pass on using?

_____
_____
_____
_____
_____
_____

What did your friends think of your drink?

_____
_____
_____
_____
_____
_____

Week 28

Go to see a live performance of a play, musical, or concert.

Watching a live performance stimulates your senses causing brain waves to synchronize, creating a social bond.

Date: ─────────

What performance did you see?

_____
_____
_____
_____
_____
_____

How did you feel after going out?

_____
_____
_____
_____
_____
_____

Has this inspired you to see more live performances?

_____
_____
_____
_____
_____
_____
_____

Week 29

Make a list of three things you love about someone special and leave it where they will find it.

*I like not only to be loved,
but also to be told I am loved.*

~ George Eliot

Date: ───────

What was on your list?

_____
_____
_____
_____
_____
_____

Where did you leave the list?

_____
_____
_____
_____
_____
_____

What was their reaction to the list?

_____
_____
_____
_____
_____
_____
_____
_____

Week 30

Take a moment to be grateful for the things in your romantic relationship that spark joy.

Studies have shown that focusing on yourself through mindfulness improves your overall wellbeing and alleviates stress.

Date: ─────────

What were you grateful for?

_____
_____
_____
_____
_____
_____

Did you share those thoughts?

_____
_____
_____
_____
_____
_____

Did it encourage you to think differently about your relationship?

_____
_____
_____
_____
_____
_____

Week 31

Do something new and exciting - take dance lessons, try indoor rock climbing, or learn to fly a trapeze!

Learning a new skill can boost your self-confidence and make you feel sexier.

Date: ―――――――

What did you do?

_____
_____
_____
_____
_____
_____

Do you want to do it again?

_____
_____
_____
_____
_____
_____

Did this inspire you to try other new activities?

_____
_____
_____
_____
_____
_____
_____

Week 32

Choose a romantic quote you love and
add it to your email signature.

We are asleep until we fall in love!

~ Leo Tolstoy

Date: —————————

What quote did you chose? Were there any you decided not to use?

_____
_____
_____
_____
_____
_____

Did anyone comment on it?

_____
_____
_____
_____
_____

Did seeing it every time you sent an email inspire you?

_____
_____
_____
_____
_____
_____

Week 33

Put a red lightbulb in a bedroom lamp, or cover a lamp with a sheer red scarf.

Love inspires, illuminates, designates and leads the way.

~ Mary Baker Eddy

Date: ───────

Did the red light make you feel more attractive?

_____
_____
_____
_____
_____

Did the red light change the mood in the bedroom?

_____
_____
_____
_____
_____

Are you going to keep the red light in the lamp year round?

_____
_____
_____
_____
_____
_____

Week 34

Enjoy a sunset with a glass of wine or your favorite tea.

A recent study showed that women who drank one to two glasses of red wine daily had a higher sex drive than those who didn't drink any wine at all.

Date: ─────────

Where did you watch the sunset?

_____
_____
_____
_____
_____
_____

What were you drinking?

_____
_____
_____
_____
_____
_____

How did it make you feel the rest of the night?

_____
_____
_____
_____
_____
_____

Week 35

Reenact your favorite scene from a romantic movie or TV show.

Romance is the deepest thing in life. It is deeper than reality.

~ Gilbert K. Chesterton

Date: ———————

What scene did you act out?

_____
_____
_____
_____
_____
_____

How did it make you feel?

_____
_____
_____
_____
_____
_____

Are there other movies or TV shows you'd now like to act out?

_____
_____
_____
_____
_____
_____
_____

Week 36

Give someone special a "Happy to You"
gift for no specific occasion.

*Tis better to have loved and lost, than never
to have loved at all.*

~ Alfred Lord Tennyson

Date: ───────

What gift did you give?

_____
_____
_____
_____
_____

When did you give it to them?

_____
_____
_____
_____
_____

What was their reaction?

_____
_____
_____
_____
_____
_____
_____

Week 37

Eat a fancy dinner by candlelight. Use your finest table linens, silverware and dishes. Then go all out with a decadent dessert.

Never close your lips to those whom you have already opened your heart.

~ Charles Dickens

Date: ──────────

What did you serve for dinner?

_____
_____
_____
_____
_____
_____

Did it make you feel more special than when eating a regular dinner?

_____
_____
_____
_____
_____
_____

Do you want to make this kind of dinner a regular thing?

_____
_____
_____
_____
_____
_____

Week 38

Tell someone special that you love them
while looking deep into their eyes.
Hold eye contact the entire time.

When two lovers stare into each other's eyes,
their heartbeats will synchronize after
about three minutes.

Date: ———

How did it make you feel doing this?

_____
_____
_____
_____
_____
_____

What was their reaction to your deep look?

_____
_____
_____
_____
_____
_____

Were you surprised by how they reacted, or how you felt doing it?

_____
_____
_____
_____
_____
_____

Week 39

Turn up the music and dance to your favorite songs. Dance like nobody's watching!

Not only will dancing burn calories, but it can also improve mood and body image.

Date: _____

What songs did you use for your dance party?

_____
_____
_____
_____
_____

Did anyone else join in on the dancing?

_____
_____
_____
_____
_____

Did you get tired or invigorated? Were you surprised by how you felt after all that dancing?

_____
_____
_____
_____
_____

Week 40

Watch an old rom-com while snuggled up under a blanket and eating popcorn.

According to a study divorce rates were half as much for couples who watched movies about romantic relationships and talked about them afterwards.

Date: ———————

What movie did you watch?

_____
_____
_____
_____
_____
_____

What were your favorite movie night moments?

_____
_____
_____
_____
_____
_____

What other movies do you now want to watch?

_____
_____
_____
_____
_____
_____

Week 41

Write your own romantic scene for a movie or TV show.

How do I love thee? Let me count the ways. I love thee to the depths and breadth and height my soul can reach, when feeling out of sight for the ends of being and ideal grace.

~ Elizabeth Barrett Browning

Date: ―――――――

What was your scene about?

_____
_____
_____
_____
_____

Did you base it off of anything you've seen before?

_____
_____
_____
_____
_____

Did you let anyone else read it?

_____
_____
_____
_____
_____
_____

Week 42

Take a nude figure drawing class alone or with your special someone.

Desire

/də zī(ə)r/ verb

To deeply long for or wish for something

Date: ───────────

Were you surprised by the confidence of the model?

_____
_____
_____
_____
_____
_____

Was the experience exciting or uncomfortable?

_____
_____
_____
_____
_____
_____

Were you pleased with your drawings?

_____
_____
_____
_____
_____
_____
_____

Week 43

Make a list of seven sexy things to say to your special someone and say one of them before bed every night this week.

According to one study, words and phrases with deeper emotional meanings, such as "I love you," receive a much better response when whispered into a person's left ear as opposed to their right ear.

Date: ───────

What was on your list?

What reaction did you get when saying them?

Which one got the best response?

Week 44

Look at yourself in the mirror, pick what body part you like the best, and flaunt it all week long.

Every night and every morning, close your eyes and take three deep breaths and say out loud "I love my life, I love my body, I love myself."

Date: ───────

What body part did you choose?

_____
_____
_____
_____
_____
_____

Did anyone comment on it?

_____
_____
_____
_____
_____
_____

Did this week inspire you to flaunt any other body parts?

_____
_____
_____
_____
_____
_____
_____

Week 45

When you make the bed, add little chocolates or a flower on your bed pillows.

A person that makes the first move is often considered more attractive to their potential partner.

Date: ───────────

What did you put on the bed?

_____
_____
_____
_____
_____
_____

Did it make going to bed feel more special?

_____
_____
_____
_____
_____
_____

Thinking of putting any other treats on the bed?

_____
_____
_____
_____
_____
_____

Week 46

Create a sexy-time playlist of songs that'll get you in the mood and keep you there.

The most common sexual fantasy, which as actually shared by both men and women, is to have sex in a romantic location. 84.9% of women fantasize about this, and 78.4% of men do too, making it the most common sexual fantasy when looking at both genders together.

Date: ⎯⎯⎯⎯⎯⎯⎯⎯

What songs were on the list?

⎯⎯

Which ones were the favorites?

⎯⎯

Which ones got the best reactions?

⎯⎯

Week 47

Have a teenage style slumber party; snuggle up in sleeping bags with flashlights and snacks.

Romance is always young.

~ John Greenleaf Whittier

Date: ———————

What was your favorite part of the night?

_____
_____
_____
_____
_____
_____
_____
_____
_____

Did it make you feel like a kid again?

_____
_____
_____
_____
_____
_____
_____
_____
_____
_____

Week 48

Buy or pick a bunch of flowers and put them somewhere you'll see them every day.

One study showed that seeing flowers first thing in the morning increased happiness, gave a boost in energy and decreased anxiety.

Date: _____

What kind of flowers did you have, and where did you put them?

_____
_____
_____
_____
_____
_____
_____
_____
_____
_____

How did seeing, and smelling fresh flowers make you feel?

_____
_____
_____
_____
_____
_____
_____
_____
_____
_____

Week 49

Spray lavender scented mist in your bedroom before going to sleep.

Romance

/rōˈmans/ noun

A physical and/or emotional feeling of excitement associated with love

Date: ───────

How did the scent make you feel? Relaxed or invigorated?

_____
_____
_____
_____
_____
_____

Where did you spray the mist?

_____
_____
_____
_____
_____
_____

Have you thought about using other scents now?

_____
_____
_____
_____
_____
_____
_____

Week 50

Write an original love poem or copy one
you really like, then post it somewhere
you'll see it every day.

There is the same difference in a person
before and after he is in love, as there is in an
unlighted lamp and one that is burning.

~ Vincent Van Gogh

Date: ───────

What is your poem?

───────────────────────────
───────────────────────────
───────────────────────────
───────────────────────────
───────────────────────────
───────────────────────────

Where did you post it?

───────────────────────────
───────────────────────────
───────────────────────────
───────────────────────────
───────────────────────────

How did the poem inspire you?

───────────────────────────
───────────────────────────
───────────────────────────
───────────────────────────
───────────────────────────
───────────────────────────
───────────────────────────

Week 51

Choose a favorite character from a romantic movie and pretend to be that person for the night.

Research has shown that being in love inspires creativity.

Date: ―――――――――

Who was the character and what was the movie?

―――――――――――――――――――――――――――――
―――――――――――――――――――――――――――――
―――――――――――――――――――――――――――――
―――――――――――――――――――――――――――――
―――――――――――――――――――――――――――――
―――――――――――――――――――――――――――――

Did pretending to be that character change how you behaved the rest of the week?

―――――――――――――――――――――――――――――
―――――――――――――――――――――――――――――
―――――――――――――――――――――――――――――
―――――――――――――――――――――――――――――
―――――――――――――――――――――――――――――
―――――――――――――――――――――――――――――

Are there other characters you want to pretend to be?

―――――――――――――――――――――――――――――
―――――――――――――――――――――――――――――
―――――――――――――――――――――――――――――
―――――――――――――――――――――――――――――
―――――――――――――――――――――――――――――
―――――――――――――――――――――――――――――

Week 52

Put a scrapbook together of all your favorite romantic moments.

I love you not only for what you are, but for what I am when I am with you.

~ Mary Carolyn Davies

Date: ———————

Did you have a favorite moment?

_____
_____
_____
_____
_____
_____

Did you show anyone the scrapbook?

_____
_____
_____
_____
_____
_____

Are there any favorite moments from this year you'd like to do again?

_____
_____
_____
_____
_____
_____

Personal Notes:

Thank you for choosing us for your journaling experience!

And congratulations to you for completing the first steps towards creating the romance-filled life of your dreams!

If you enjoyed this journal, check out all the other versions we have coming up at:

www.52weekjournal.com

www.ingramcontent.com/pod-product-compliance
Lightning Source LLC
Chambersburg PA
CBHW020912080526
44589CB00011B/556